XTREME UNIVERSE

QUASARS

AND MORE DAZZLING DISCOVERIES

A&D Xtreme
BOLD HI-LO NONFICTION
An imprint of Abdo Publishing
abdobooks.com

ANN WILLIAMS

TAKE IT TO THE XTREME!

GET READY FOR AN EXTREME ADVENTURE! THE PAGES OF THIS BOOK WILL TAKE YOU INTO THE THRILLING WORLD OF ASTRONOMICAL WONDERS. WHEN YOU HAVE FINISHED READING THIS BOOK, TAKE THE XTREME CHALLENGE ON PAGE 45 ABOUT WHAT YOU'VE LEARNED!

ABDOBOOKS.COM
Published by Abdo Publishing, a division of ABDO, PO Box 398166, Minneapolis, Minnesota 55439.

Printed in the United States of America, North Mankato, MN.
102024
012025

THIS BOOK CONTAINS RECYCLED MATERIALS

Design: Kelly Doudna, Mighty Media, Inc.
Production: Mighty Media, Inc.
Editor: Katherine Chu

Cover Photograph: International Gemini Observatory/NOIRLab/NSF/AURA/P. Marenfeld
Interior Photographs: Bettymaya Foott, NRAO/AUI/NSF, pp. 12–13; ESA/Hubble & NASA/D. Milisavljevic (Purdue University), pp. 8–9; ESO/Digitized Sky Survey 2/Dark Energy Survey, pp. 22–23; ESO/M. Kornmesser, pp. 18–19, 24–25; ESO/VPHAS+ team. Acknowledgment: Cambridge Astronomical Survey Unit, pp. 26–27; I. Plauchu-Frayn, pp. 40–41; International Gemini Observatory/AURA/Lynette Cook, p. 44; International Gemini Observatory/NOIRLab/NSF/AURA/P. Marenfeld, p. 1; James Steidl/Shutterstock Images, pp. 16–17; Jin Ma, Beijing Planetarium, pp. 28–29; Kim et al. (2020), EHT Collaboration, pp. 14–15; KPNO/NOIRLab/IAU/SKAO/NSF/AURA/R. Sparks, pp. 42–43; M. Tzukran, p. 40; NASA, ESA and G. Bacon (STScI), pp. 32–33; NASA, ESA, H. Bond (STScI), and M. Barstow (University of Leicester), p. 33; NASA/JPL, pp. 38–39; NASA/JPL-Caltech, pp. 10–11, 20–21, 36–37; NASA/JPL-Caltech/GSFC, pp. 30–31; NASA/JPL-Caltech/Roma Tre Univ., pp. 6–7; NASA/JPL/USGS, pp. 34–35; NOIRLab/NSF/AURA/J. da Silva, pp. 4–5; Wikimedia Commons, p. 16
Design Elements: Arafat/Adobe Stock (header background); pixel/Adobe Stock (universe); Sergey Nivens/Shutterstock Images (header background)

LIBRARY OF CONGRESS CONTROL NUMBER: 2024938313
PUBLISHER'S CATALOGING-IN-PUBLICATION DATA
Names: Williams, Ann, author.
Title: Quasars and more dazzling discoveries / by Ann Williams
Description: Minneapolis, Minnesota : ABDO Publishing, 2025 | Series: Xtreme universe | Includes online resources and index.
Identifiers: ISBN 9781098295073 (lib. bdg.) | ISBN 9798384915126 (ebook)
Subjects: LCSH: Quasars--Juvenile literature. | Active galactic nuclei--Juvenile literature. | Black holes (Astronomy)--Juvenile literature. | Universe--Juvenile literature. | Outer space--Exploration--Juvenile literature. | Astronomy--Juvenile literature.
Classification: DDC 523.112--dc23

CONTENTS

CHAPTER 1

DISTANT YET BRIGHT

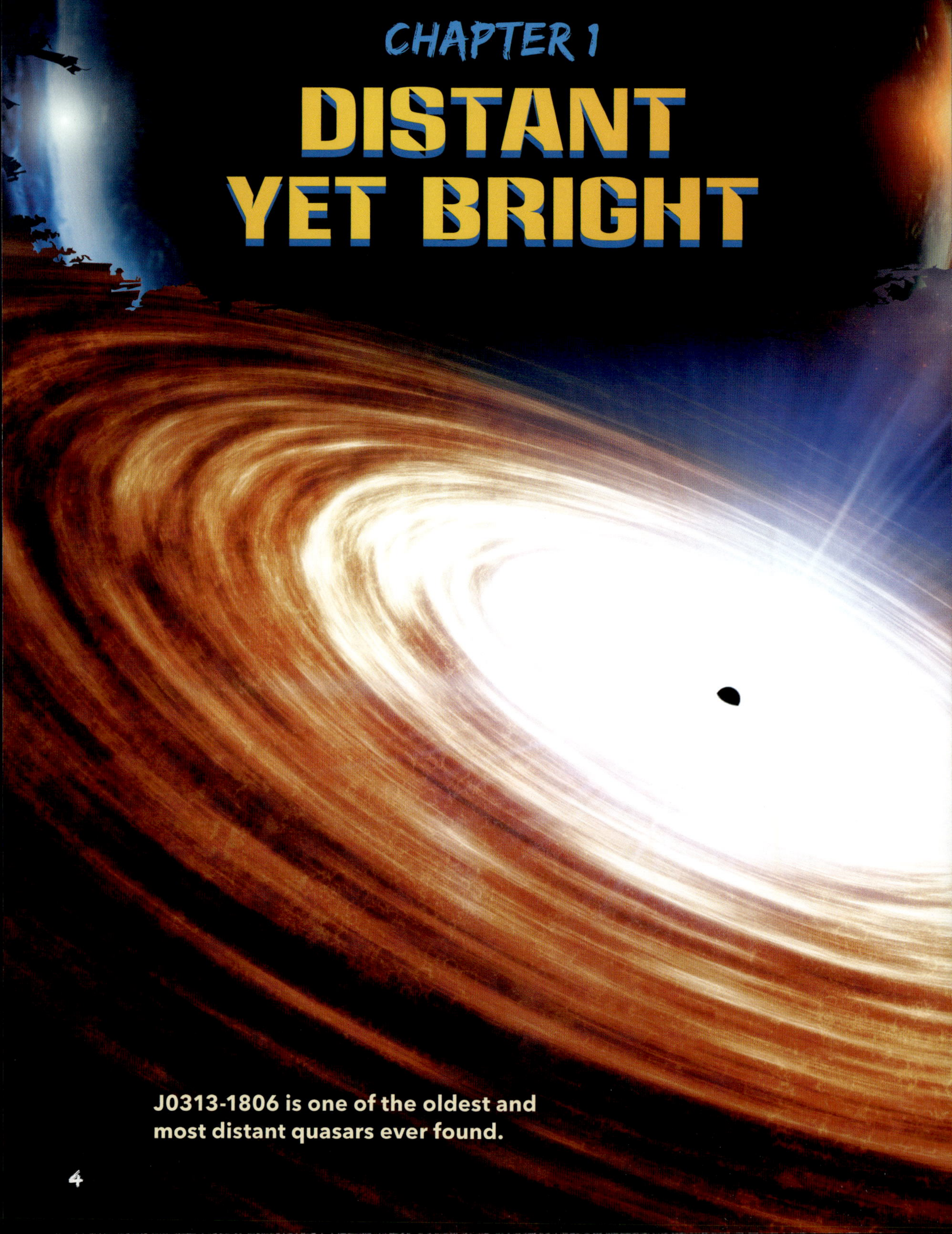

J0313-1806 is one of the oldest and most distant quasars ever found.

Looking up at the night sky, you might see many small, bright lights. These are faraway space objects! They include stars, **meteoroids**, planets, and **comets**.

But the brightest objects are in the farthest reaches of space. They can't be seen by the naked eye. The brightest objects in the universe are quasars!

CHAPTER 2

WHAT IS A QUASAR?

Quasars form around **supermassive** black holes. A black hole is an area with such strong gravity that nothing can escape it. Not even light can escape a black hole. Black holes that have especially strong gravity are called supermassive black holes.

Galaxy NGC 1068 (*pink swirl*) has a supermassive black hole and quasar at its center.

Supermassive black holes are constantly consuming everything around them. Sometimes, a black hole pulls matter so fast that it can't all enter the black hole at the same time. This causes a backup of matter outside the black hole.

Galaxy NGC 7331 and its supermassive black hole. Most galaxies have supermassive black holes at their centers.

The matter getting pulled into the black hole forms a spinning disk. The **particles** in the disk crash into one another at high speeds. This causes them to get **extremely** hot and glow very brightly.

The **supermassive** black hole and its disk of hot gas make up the center of newly forming **galaxies**. This center region is known as a quasar.

Quasars also shoot out long jets of extremely bright energy.

CHAPTER 3

OBSERVING QUASARS

The Karl G. Jansky Very Large Array in New Mexico has 28 radio telescopes.

Quasars are so far away that astronomers mainly study them using radio telescopes. These telescopes have an antenna and a receiver that detect radio waves in space. The information is sent to a computer, which creates an image of the object that **emitted** the radio waves.

Radio astronomy was developed in the 1950s. At the time, astronomers mostly used radio telescopes to observe **galaxies**. During their observations, they saw some objects that looked like stars. Radio astronomers called these objects "quasi-stellar radio sources." This was later shortened to "quasar." However, they didn't know what quasars actually were.

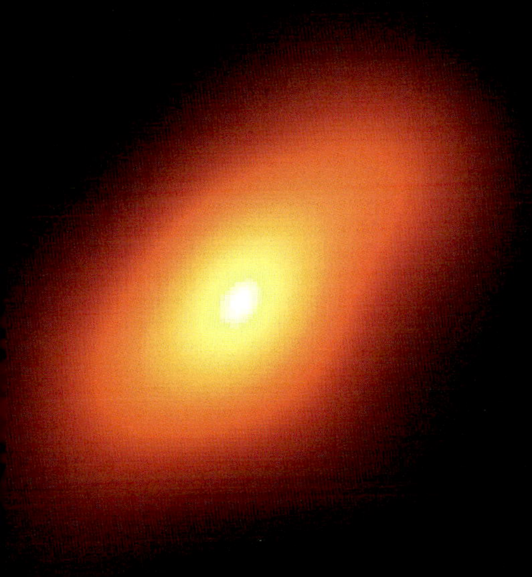

In 2020, astronomers observed Quasar 3C 279 (*above*) and its black hole shooting out streams of hot gas (*below*).

CHAPTER 4

MAARTEN SCHMIDT

Schmidt (*inset*) measured the distance to a quasar at the Palomar Observatory (*background*) near San Diego, California.

In the 1960s, Dutch-born American astronomer Maarten Schmidt was studying quasars. He was the first to measure the exact distance to a quasar. It was 2.5 **billion** light-years from Earth!

XTREME FACT

A light-year is the distance light travels in one year. One light-year equals about 5.88 trillion miles (9.46 trillion km).

Schmidt also noticed signs that the quasar he was studying was moving farther away. This meant quasars were bright enough to be detected from very far away. In fact, they were brighter than any stars scientists had observed.

Astronomers continued to study quasars and realized that they were coming from black holes deep in space. Because of this, many **experts** think that quasars eventually become new **galaxies**.

XTREME FACT

It can take more than 1 billion years for a galaxy to form.

Quasar ULAS J1120+0641 was discovered in 2011. Its black hole has a mass that is 2 billion times greater than the sun's.

Schmidt's work also supported the big bang **theory** of how the universe began. The big bang theory was proposed in the 1920s and further developed in the 1940s. It says that the universe started from one huge explosion and has been **expanding** ever since. New **galaxies** forming and moving outward supports the idea that the universe is continuing to grow.

Astronomers found that quasar winds create a lot of space dust.

CHAPTER 5

THE BRIGHTEST OF THE BRIGHT

The region where J0529-4351 is located. Astronomers used the Siding Spring Observatory in New South Wales, Australia, and the European Southern Observatory's Very Large Telescope in Chile to identify J0529-4351.

In February 2024, astronomers at Australian National University in Canberra, Australia, identified a new quasar. It was 12 **billion** light-years from Earth and called J0529-4351. As of 2024, it was the biggest and brightest quasar ever discovered. That made J0529-4351 the brightest object in the universe!

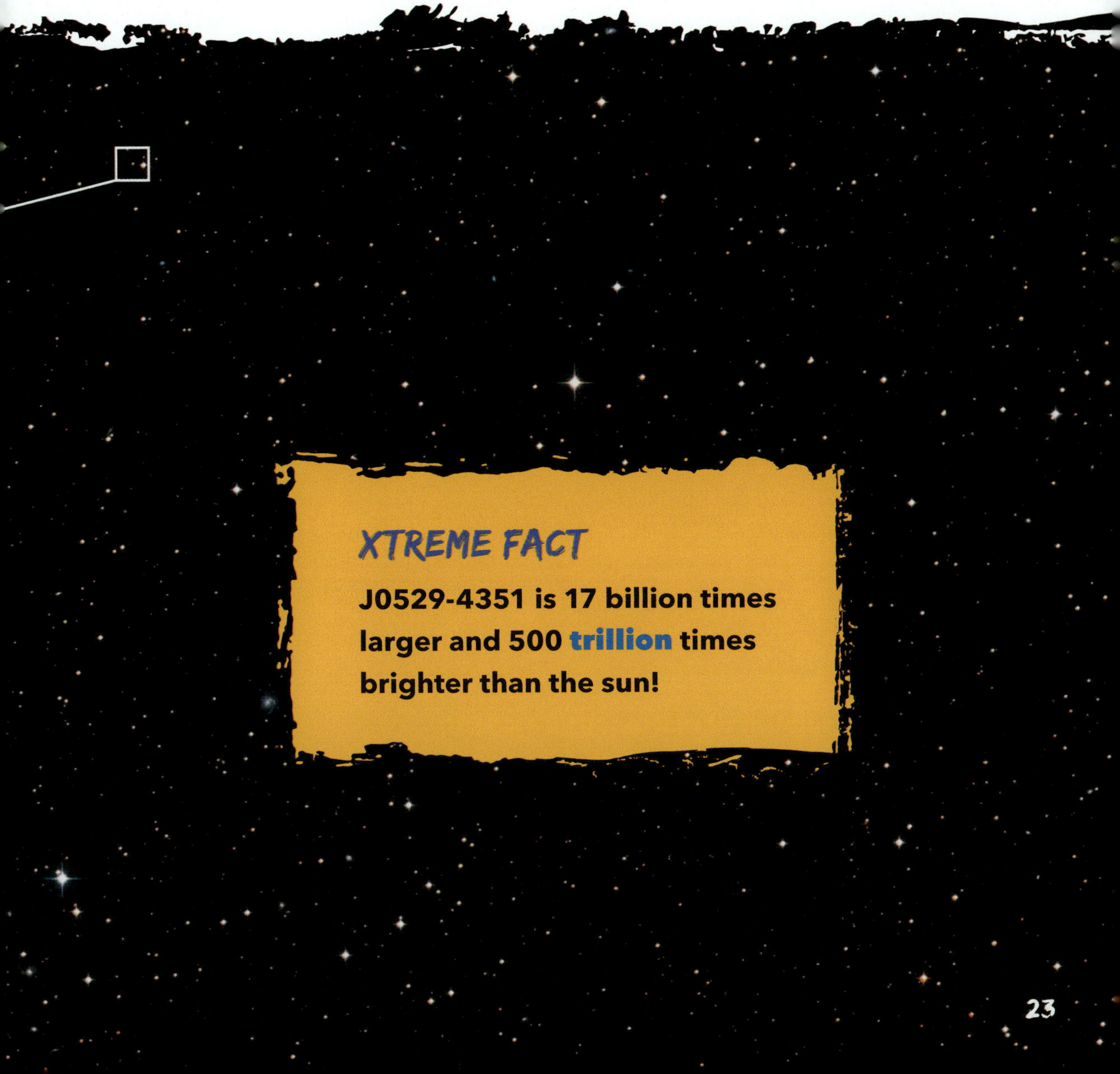

XTREME FACT

J0529-4351 is 17 billion times larger and 500 trillion times brighter than the sun!

The amount of matter J0529-4351's black hole sucks in each day is equal to the sun's mass.

The **supermassive** black hole that created J0529-4351 is the fastest-growing black hole ever observed. Astronomers are continuing to study J0529-4351 and its black hole. They think learning about these space objects will help them better understand the universe.

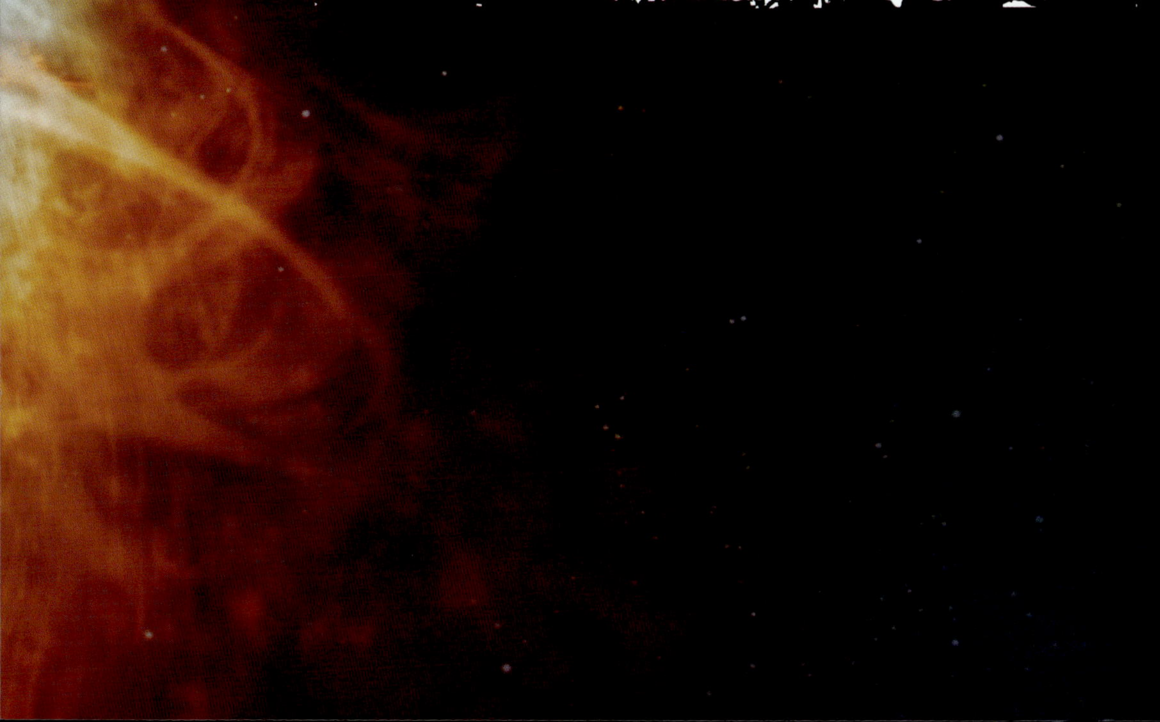

CHAPTER 6

BRIGHTEST EXPLOSIONS

Besides quasars, the universe contains many other **extremely** bright objects. One of the brightest is a supernova. A supernova is an explosion that happens when a large star **collapses** and dies. Supernovas are the biggest explosions humans have ever observed.

XTREME FACT

It is unlikely that the sun will become a supernova because it's too small.

The Vela supernova remnant. A supernova remnant is what remains after a star explodes into a supernova.

ASASSN-15lh is known as a superluminous supernova. This is because it's much brighter than a normal supernova.

Astronomers discovered the brightest known supernova in 2015. It is called ASASSN-15lh and is about 3.8 **billion** light-years from Earth. ASASSN-15lh is 200 times brighter than most supernovas. No one knows why it's so much brighter than other supernovas. But astronomers continue to study ASASSN-15lh to find the answer.

CHAPTER 7

THE SUN AND OTHER STARS

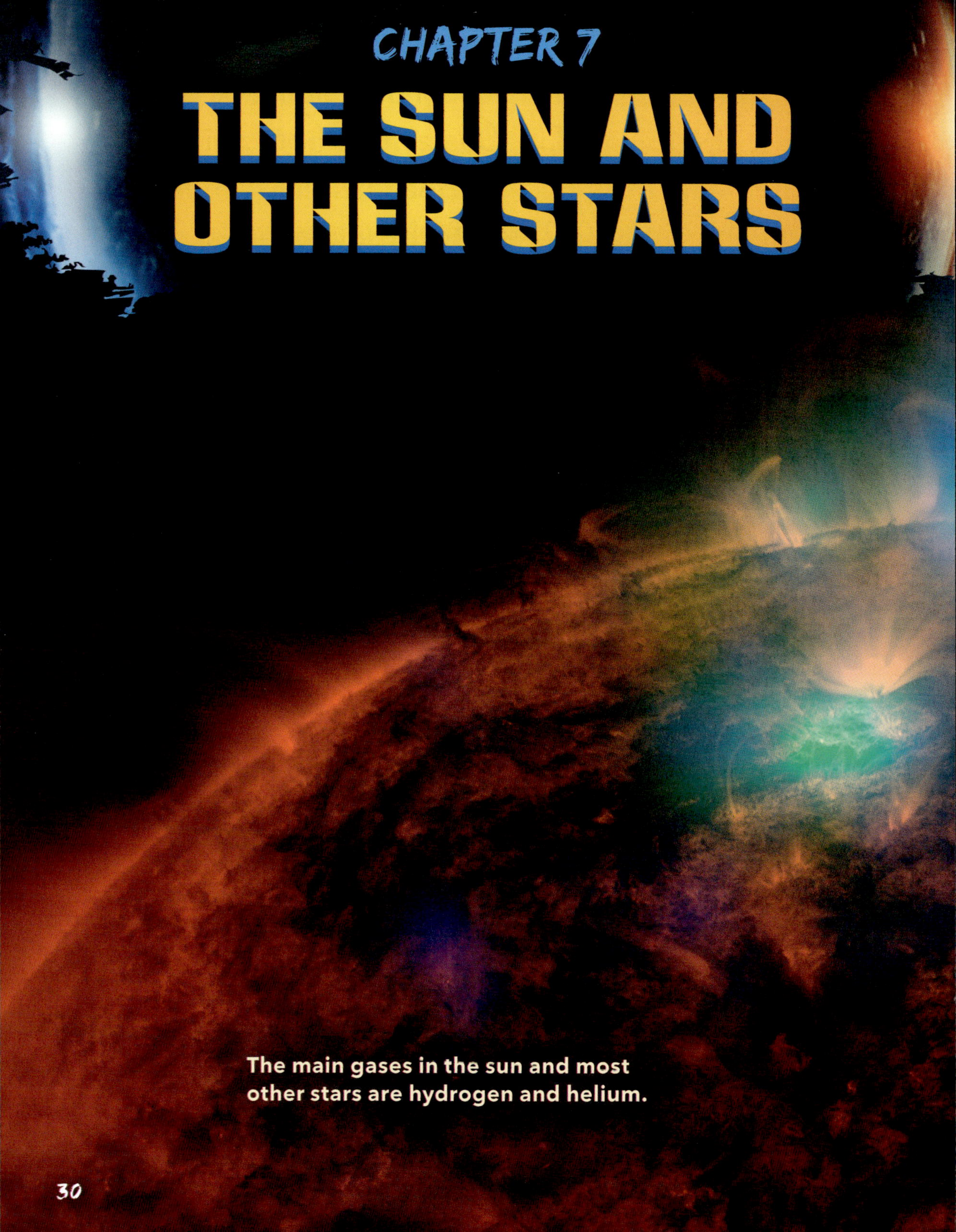

The main gases in the sun and most other stars are hydrogen and helium.

Stars are also very bright space objects. A star is a giant ball of gas. Earth's sun is a star. It seems very big and bright because it's the closest star to Earth. But there are many bigger, brighter stars in space.

The brightest star in the night sky is Sirius A. It is 8.6 light-years from Earth. Because it's so bright, Sirius A is easy to see, even without a telescope. It is almost twice as big as the sun and 25 times brighter.

Sirius A is also called the Dog Star. This is because it's part of the constellation *Canis Major*, which is Latin for "the greater dog."

An image of Sirius A (*center*) and its companion star Sirius B (*lower left*) taken by the Hubble Space Telescope.

CHAPTER 8

BRIGHT REFLECTIONS

Some space objects are bright even though they don't make their own light. The brightest of these objects visible from Earth is the moon. The moon can look very bright because it reflects the sun's light.

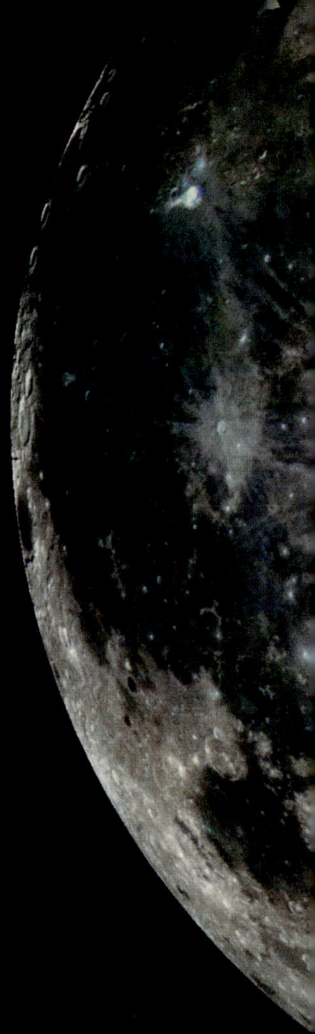

Though the moon may look white from Earth, it's actually different shades of dark gray.

Planets also reflect light from the sun. The brightest planet visible from Earth is Venus. It is the planet closest to Earth. Venus is also **extremely** reflective. It reflects most of the light that the sun shines on it.

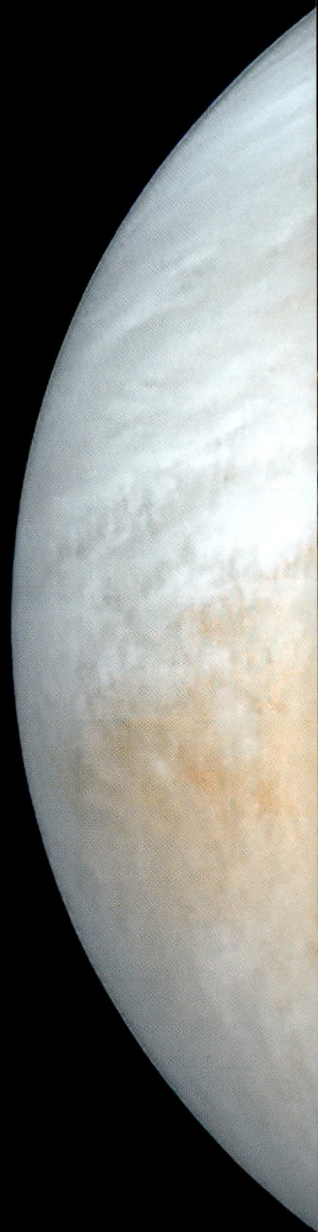

Venus is sometimes called Earth's sister planet. It is about the same size as Earth and may have supported life billions of years ago.

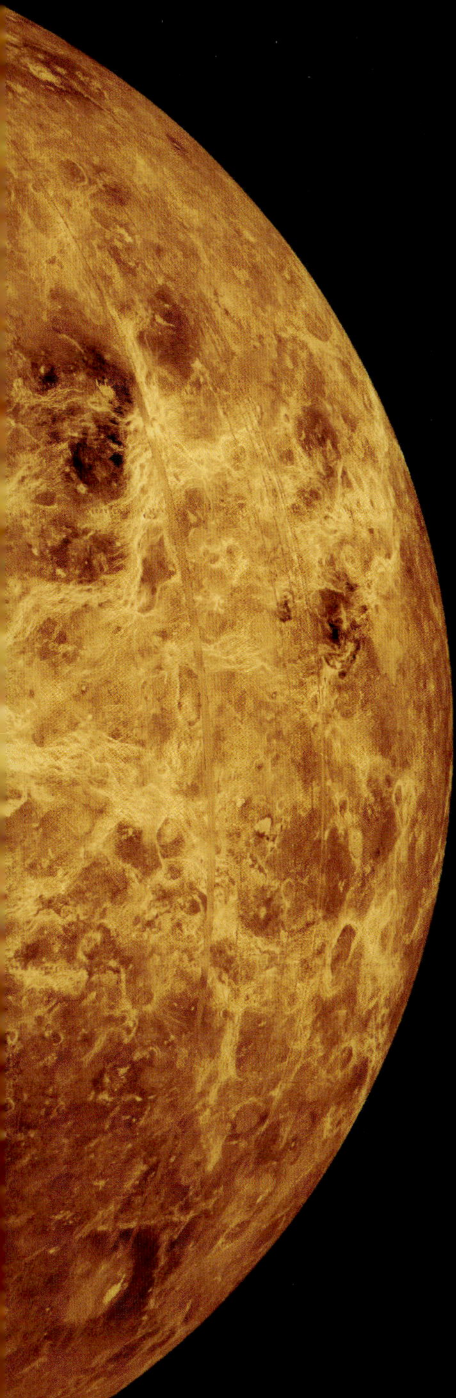

The gas in Venus's atmosphere traps some of the sun's heat. This makes the surface of Venus very hot. Venus is the hottest planet in the solar system, even though it is not the closest to the sun.

XTREME FACT

The surface of Venus is so hot that it melts metal, even lead.

Venus is about 870 degrees Fahrenheit (466°C).

CHAPTER 9

HUMANMADE BRIGHTNESS

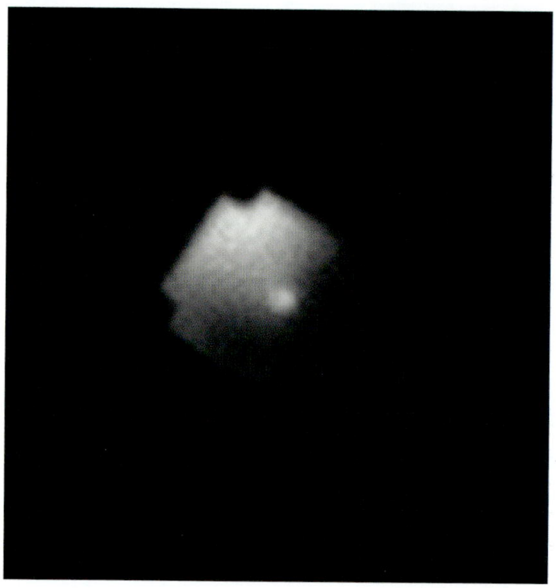

A photo of BlueWalker 3 taken from Earth. BlueWalker 3 is 693 square feet (64 sq m) large.

Not all bright objects in space are natural. Some were made by humans and **launched** into space. Many artificial objects in space are **satellites**. In 2022, the BlueWalker 3 communications satellite was launched. It is the brightest satellite. The brightness comes from the sun's light reflecting off the satellite's large antenna **array**.

A trail of light left by BlueWalker 3

Large **satellites**, such as BlueWalker 3, sometimes block the view of natural space objects. This makes it difficult for astronomers to study natural space objects using Earth-based telescopes. And, the brightness of satellites causes **light pollution**. This makes it harder to see **constellations** and other objects in the night sky.

BlueWalker 3 creates a bright trail of light, which can block astronomers' observations. It also transmits strong radio signals, which can cause problems for radio astronomers.

CHAPTER 10

SHINING BRIGHT

There are many bright objects in the universe. These include quasars, supernovas, stars, and more. Astronomers study these objects to learn more about the universe and how it formed. They also work with **satellite** companies and the government to reduce the effect of artificial satellites on observations of space.

An illustration of Quasar ULAS. Because it's impossible to see some space objects directly, artists create illustrations of what they may look like.

XTREME CHALLENGE

TAKE THE QUIZ BELOW AND PUT WHAT YOU'VE LEARNED TO THE TEST!

1) What is a quasar?

2) What do astronomers use to study quasars?

3) When was the big bang theory first proposed?

4) What is the brightest star in the night sky?

5) Would you rather study space or help launch satellites that could help people on Earth?

GLOSSARY

array–a large number or group.

billion–the number 1,000,000,000, or one thousand million.

collapse–to suddenly break down or to cave in.

comet–a mass of ice and dust that moves through space and develops a tail as it nears the sun.

constellation–a group of stars that together form a pattern or shape.

emit–to give off or out.

expand–to get bigger.

expert–a person very knowledgeable about a certain subject.

extremely–to a degree that exceeds the ordinary or expected.

galaxy–a very large group of stars, planets, and other objects in space.

launch–to send a spacecraft into space.

light pollution–bright light that comes from artificial outdoor light at night.

meteoroid—rocky pieces that have broken off comets, asteroids, and planets.

particle—a very small piece of matter, such as an atom or molecule.

satellite—a manufactured object that orbits and relays scientific information back to Earth.

supermassive—having a very large amount of mass.

theory—a general rule offered to explain a scientific event.

trillion—the number 1,000,000,000,000, or one thousand billion.

ONLINE RESOURCES

INDEX